pocke
oceanside

jeanine deegan

contents

1. WELCOME TO OCEANSIDE 1
2. TRIP PLANNING 4
   - getting here 4
   - car 5
3. NOTES 7
4. LET'S HAVE SOME FUN 8
   - beaches 9
   - surf schools in oceanside 13
   - harbor activities 14
5. NOTES 19
6. ATTRACTIONS 20
7. NOTES 22
8. EATING AND DRINKING IN O'SIDE 23
   - top restaurants 23
   - Breakfasts and coffee houses 26
   - Breweries and bars 28
9. NOTES 31
10. GOLF COURSES 32
11. NOTES 34
12. THINGS TO DO 35
    - Market day 35

	Visit Mission San Luis Rey	36
	Cruise bike trails	36
	Take a hike	38

13. NOTES 43

	goodbye and please come again	45
	Bibliography	47
	NOTES	53

Copyright © 2022 by Jeanine Fagan All rights reserved.

No part of this book may be reproduced in any form or by any electronic or mechanical means, including information storage and retrieval systems, without written permission from the author, except for the use of brief quotations in a book review.

Created with Vellum

Created with Vellum

welcome to oceanside

...

...

WHILE IN COLLEGE in San Diego, I often visited my friend stationed in Oceanside. A 40-minute drive from college life to this relaxing coastal community made it the perfect getaway from college chaos. About ten years ago, I was deter-
Jeanine Deegan

mined to buy a place in North County near my besties who had settled in the community just after the coast guard tour and the college roomy who became a professor in North County San Diego. Today as I write, I am nestled in a beachfront condo listening to the waves crash outside my sliding door.

The peaceful sounds of the ocean are something I hope will calm your soul when you visit this old-style beach town boasting California fun and sun without the crowds of other beach towns. O'side is a casual coastal community with a history rooted in buildings, the pier, and generations of families that have called this place home for years. O'side New England Harbor has shops and restaurants and is the launching point for many water adventures. Oceanside's pier is the longest wooden pier on the west coast, measuring 1,954 feet long.

This guide will help you plan your vacation and provide information to organize your time here. Write your thoughts in the notes section. You can open it up in the morning to plan your day, carry it in your pocket as you head out on afternoon excursions, and consult it again to plan your dinner venue. I hope it makes your trip to Southern California easier and provides you with some useful tips on your vacation. Let's get going and enjoy a great time at one of SoCal's premier coastal towns.

trip planning

...

...

geting here

AS YOU PLAN YOUR VACATION, use the notes section at the end of the book to write your ideas, your reservations confirmations, and keep a checklist. It will all be with you as part of this guide, so there is no need for the Manilla folders with lots of notes. It can all be located in this easy-to-carry book.

Flights

Nestled on the coast 36 miles north of San Diego Airport (SAN), 50 miles south of John Wayne Orange County Airport (SNA), or 90 miles from Los Angeles International Airport (LAX), there are lots of options to choose from for your air travel.

I suggest using a search engine to shop for flights to

accommodate your budget. A few favorites are Kayak or Skyscanner. In addition to flight costs, be sure to consider the travel time from your airport. Travel time in California is delayed during work commutes, especially on Fridays. So, for example, if you are planning a flight that arrives at LAX on a Friday at 4:00 pm, you can predict a commute twice the time one usually would expect on a 90-mile freeway trip. Not surprising, when we add the population of Los Angeles County, Orange County, and San Diego County, there are more than 16 million residents. The total state has about 39 million residents making California the most populated state in the United States.

car
Rental Car vs. Uber, Lyft, or Bus

Gasoline in California is usually very high so you may consider traveling by bus or hiring a car to drive you from the airport, then getting around with public transportation and uber. However, renting a car is probably better if your vacation includes several excursions to visit San Diego attractions, Disneyland, or Knotts Berry Farm. You may find discounts bundled with your flights or use another search engine, such as Priceline or Kayak , to find the right car for you. If you are adventurous and want to try a particular vehicle or electric car, you can go through Turo.com.

Another option is to take a bus or shuttle from the airport to Oceanside, then rent your car at a local car rental agency in Oceanside. Some easy-to-access rental car agencies in Oceanside are

Enterprise
875 S. Coast Hwy, Oceanside, CA 92054
(760)966-9090
Jeanine Deegan

Budget
1771 S Oceanside Blvd Ste B, Oceanside, CA
(760) 757-5799
Hertz 1816 C Oceanside Blvd. Oceanside, CA
(760) 722-7031

notes
...

let's have some fun

...

...

NOW THAT YOU ARE SCHEDULED, have a place to stay, and are packed, let's get going! Assuming you have talked to your friends, children, or travel partners, it's time to select a few sites and activities. There is a lot to do, but you can pick when you want to be busy, chill, and commune with the beach or enjoy a nature hike. Included are some activities depending on your preferences for Active or Chill adventures.

beaches

Sand Man

The beaches of Oceanside provide hours of fun for the family. There are 3 miles of beach, but frankly, the best sand is found near the pier. As you perch your beach blanket and stake your umbrella, you will see that O'Sides finest lifeguards protect you. The guards are only on duty from Memorial weekend to Labor Day, so if the waters are choppy while you are there other times of the year, please be careful. Here in O'side, we call our beaches by their locations. Depending on your vibe for the day, the crowds, and the tide, you may select different beaches all within the 3 miles of Oceanside shoreline.

Starting with our most northern area, Harbor beach, to our most southern shore, butting up to Carlsbad called Cassidy St. Beach, all have different charms and rest upon changing sand bases depending on the season and sand erosion.

- **Pier View North:** provides lots of sand, but parking is a block away.
- **Pier View South:** directly below the resorts and can be a great spot if you want to add a pier stroke or perch on a green park at **Tyson Park**.
- **Tyson Beach:** sits just below the park, so you can enjoy both simultaneously. Parking is available just up from the beaches.
- **Oceanside Blvd** and **Wisconsin Street Beaches** are usually less crowded because the sand is often not plentiful unless the tides are out. Paid Parking is available a block away near the railroad tracks and on the streets.
- **Buccaneer Beach** is a fun family spot because it has another great park that hosts a delicious small outdoor cafe called Buccaneer cafe. More on this in our food section. Parking is open at the park but will get crowded during the day, so get there early if you want a spot.

- **Cassidy Beach** is the most southern beach in Oceanside. As you approach it heading West you will travel under the iconic S.O'side Cassidy street bridge.
- **Harbor Beach.** This beach is north of the San Luis
- Rey River bed and is the beach side of the harbor. If you are interested in surfing, **Pier View North** and **South** will provide some sound waves, but for a different and less crowded experience, you may want to head North and hang ten from **Harbor Beach.** Jetties protect this beach, so the sand is vast, and the waves are reliable. There is parking if you get there early and lots of bathrooms.
- **Dog Beach.**

Jeanine Deegan

Enjoying Del Mar Dog Beach

Although Oceanside canine lovers are working diligently to have one of the O'side beaches deemed a dog beach at the time of printing, we do not have a designated dog beach. Dogs are allowed on sidewalks and parks as long as they are leached. Please utilize doggy bags for your dog's duty because nobody likes stepping in that stuff. Additionally, the bacteria from this excrement can cause severe contamination of our coastal waters. Although Oceanside can't brag about a dog beach yet, we suggest our visitors take their energetic four-legged animals to Del Mar, where they will have a blast running in the surf with other four-legged friends.

Del Mar Dog Beach3902 29th St. Del Mar, CA 92014

1. This beach is about 25 minutes south in the city of Del Mar.
2. Take the five south exit Via De La Valle in San Diego.
3. Follow Via De La Valle and Camino Del Mar to Ocean Front in Del Mar
4. Use the right two lanes to turn right onto Via De La Valle
5. Turn left onto Camino Del Mar
6. Turn right onto 29th St.
7. 29th St turns left and becomes Ocean Front.
8. Doggy Beach Heaven will be on the left. It is wheelchair accessible, and some parking is available depending on visiting dogs.

Beach surfing

From one-time lessons to week-long camps, one of the surf schools listed will surely meet your needs.

Hang 10

surf schools in oceanside

1. **California Kahuna**
2. **Learn To Rip Surf Instruction**
3. **Learn To Surf With Heather Pine**
4. **Mark's Surf Instruction**
5. **North County Surf Academy**
6. **Oceanside Surf School**
7. **San Diego Surf**
8. **Surf 'N' Fire**
9. **Surf Ride Surf School**

10. **Whitlock Surf Experience**
harbor activities

Oceanside Harbor

Oceanside Harbor is a quaint New England-style village on the north side of Oceanside. If you go further north, you will be in Camp Pendleton. This bustling area is where you will rent paddleboards, jet skis, and Duffy boats, join a fishing expedition or participate in a whale and dolphin excursion. There are lots of shops and many delicious restaurants located at the harbor. If you want to venture to the end of the harbor, you will find more restaurants.

Pocket Guide to Oceanside

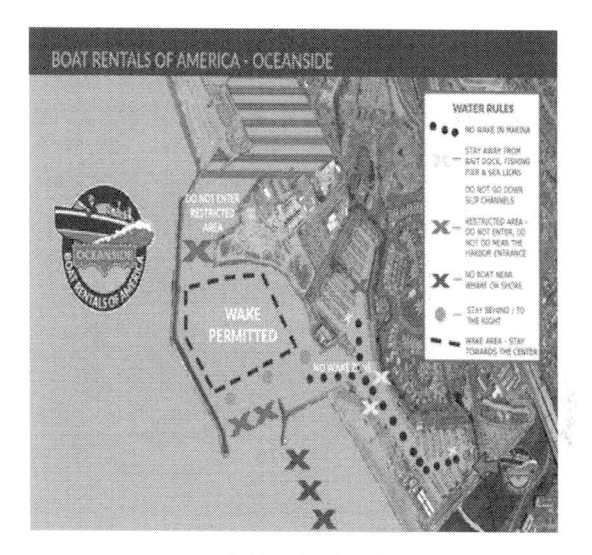

Guide to boating rules

1. **Oceanside harbor fun rentals:**
   Power boat rentals
   Paddleboards
   Jetski's
   Eight or 12-person Duffy's (electric boats)
   Kayaks single and double 855-690-079455

2. **Fishing**

   o **Oceanside Pier** fishing is an exciting way to catch your dinner and enjoy the sun on the

famous pier in Oceanside. From the pier, you can snag lots of great fish. No fishing license is needed; you can rent your gear from the Pier Bait Shop in the middle of the pier.
- **Harbor fishing** is an excellent place for beginners because of the shelter provided by the harbor. Many locals recommend the small craft harbor fishing pier a quarter of a mile beyond the Harbor shops. Here you will hear loud sea lions as you catch many fish species attracted to the calm harbor waters.

o **Boat fishing** A few companies are operating at Oceanside Harbor. This easy-to-access harbor makes day excursions or multiday trips convenient for locals and visitors. As you test your upper body strength pulling in your catch, you might be surprised to see it's an Albacore, Mahi-Mahi, Sea Bass, or even a Mako or Thresher Shark. You're sure to see some amazing sea life on the trip too.

o **Helgren's:** Helgren's Oceanside Sportfishing has been in Oceanside for over 40 years. They have several options, from multi-day trips to 3/4 day fishing trips. Helgren's has three boats ranging from 60 feet to 105 feet depending on the length of the journey. 1395 N. Harbor Dr. Oceanside, 760-722-2133

o **Fish Taxi:** Fish Taxi sportfishing is available for families and groups of up to 6 people. You will need a fishing license, but they will help you with fishing gear and even provide refreshments. 800-593-1234

o **Pacific Venture Charters:** Don't let the fear of sea sickness hold you back. The boat at Pacific Venture is equipped with innovative technology to prevent 90 percent of the roll experienced by other ships. Now even the seasick prone can enjoy the Ocean of opportunities available in the Great Pacific. These voyages are private charters designed to meet your parties' needs. You can even get the kids on a halfday trip to introduce them to the sport.760-518-5198

3. Dolphin and whale watching

o **Oceanside Adventures** Depending on the season, you will see different wildlife. An onboard nature guide will tell you about the history of Oceanside and through their expertise, will guide you to spectacular Marine life. They also offer Catamaran wine crises and will allow you to host your own private party should you want something more intimate.

o **Zodiac Expeditions:** Provides an exhilarating sea adventure on a six-person zodiac vessel. Captained by a USCG Licensed Captain and accredited biologist, you're sure to learn and see a lot of Marine life.

4. Sail Boat

- If you've always wanted to learn or are already a sailor, Sail Oceanside will provide your party of six with a memorable experience in Oceanside. From Sunset sails to Whale Watching or burials at sea, this voyage will surely blow you away. **Sail Oceanside** 760-804-5788

notes
...

attractions

...

...

AFTER A FEW DAYS of sun and water, you may start thinking about some different activities to partake in while on this SoCal trip. Here are a few options to debate as you plan your trip. Don't forget to look for discounted tickets through your employers, California Costco, and by visiting the Oceanside Tourist Center upon arrival. Because there are so many fun amusement parks in Southern California, they will be listed here with the approximate distance to Oceanside. You can add anticipated travel times to your decision-making process. Don't forget to use the note sections to write your decisions, keep track of reservations, etc. **Things to do South of Oceanside**

San Diego County boasts several great day visits. Below are the most popular. As you vacation in Oceanside year after year, you will experience the many attractions of SoCal. Don't try it all on your first trip to O'side because while in California; you want to relax and get the California vibe going.

Pocket Guide to Oceanside

Worry less: no stress. Or possibly the South of the Border motto "Manana."

1. Legoland: 8.0miles Legoland
2. Del Mar Fairgrounds 16 miles June-July
3. Del Mar Race Track 16 miles End of July to midSeptember
4. San Diego Zoo: 41 miles San Diego Zoo
5. San Diego Zoo Safari Park: 27 miles
6. Sea World San Diego: 36 miles Sea World
7. PETCO Park: Home of the Padres 35 miles
8. Gaslamp District: 38 miles Gaslamp District
9. Old Town:35 miles Old Town San Diego
10. Downtown San Diego 38 miles Downtown
11. Balboa Park 38 miles Balboa Park
12. Coronado Island: 36 miles Coronado

Things to do North of Oceanside

1. Angel Stadium of Anaheim, Home of the Angels,
   55 mi
2. Honda Center: Home of Ducks and venue for many concerts 55 mi
3. Disneyland California Resort: 58 miles
4. Knott's Berry Farm: 64 miles

Los Angeles

1. Hollywood Sign: 95 miles
2. Universal Studios Hollywood: 96 miles

notes
...

eating and drinking in o'side

. . .

. . .

OCEANSIDE HAS LONG PRODUCED farm-to-table menus alongside delicious Seafood and Burgers. But the past few years have created some world-class cuisines in this small Ocean community. O'siders have coined the dining experience as "Flip Flop Fine Dining," where you can experience the fresh quality of locally sourced ingredients on menus created by some of the best San Diego County chefs in a relaxed environment.

top restaurants
These are not listed in any order. Please check the sights for reservation availability and inside secrets.

1. **The Lab Collaborative**: American (new) Modern delicious farm fresh dining provided by caring staff with a menu that will sure to delight. The Lab Collaborative.Reservations through website
2. **The Piper**: American (New) The piper features fresh, handmade plates of pasta and garden-

totable delicacies in a bright, happy, California coastal

setting just off the beach. Culinary feasts await you at the Seabird, where this restaurant resides. Reservations through the website

3. **The Wrench and Rodent Seabasstropub**: Seafood with a Japanese and French twist. Locally and responsibly sourced fish and produce. Wrench and Rodent Open Table Reservations

4. **Matsu**: Modern Japanese. Fresh and local cuisine marries Japanese and Californian flavors for a unique ten-course fine dining tasting menu delivered in a 48-seat lively, and friendly dining venue. Reservations through explorestock.com

5. **Flying Pig**: Southern Charm meets Pork BBQ. The hard edge of industrial design blended with the soft edge of a county farmhouse has created a cuisine that will explode your taste buds. First come, first serve. Call ahead for large parties.

6. **The Blade 1936**: Italian. Located in the historic Blade and Tribune News Building, this upscale casual modern Italian restaurant features fresh pasta, local seafood, steaks, and sinful desserts. They also Vegan options. Reservations through Open Table

7. **Masters Kitchen and Cocktail**: American varietal on PCH serves fantastic food combined with delicious cocktails in a trendy beachy atmosphere. Reservations through the website and Open Table

8. **The Plot**: Totally Plant-Based amazing food will cause you to question why you ever ate meat. Lunch, dinner, and weekend Brunch are available. Reservations through Open Table

9. **333 Pacific**: Seafood, steak, and stunning views of Pier. Happy hour combined with cocktails and the view is a great way wrap up your day in O'side.
   Don't forget WinWednesdays for 50% off bottles. Cheers! 333 Pacific Reservations through the website.
10. **Anita's Mexican Restaurant and Cantina**: Authentic Mexican food is always a hit while visiting So.Cal. This Mexican Cantina serves classic fare and delicious margaritas in a festive environment.No reservations, but you may call ahead to check wait times.
11. **The Privateer coal-fired pizza**. The chefs at Privateer are passionate about creating fresh gourmet pizzas and appetizers. All food is made from scratch with the freshest ingredients using only locally grown greens and spices from neighboring Cyclops farms. You can order online or ahead in for a casual, delicious dining experience.
12. **Hello Betty Fish House and Roof Top Lounge:** One block off the beach, this restaurant and lounge offer respite from the sun, fish and chips, Baja-style tacos, and margaritas. Pat away the sand and head up Mission Avenue to this fish house. Although no reservations are accepted, you can call ahead if you have a big party. Take-out and private events are also welcome.
13. **Carte Blanche:** French-inspired Mexican Bistro. Providing fresh food for friends to enjoy together in a hip casual venue. Located downtown on

Cleveland Street. Open for Brunch at 11:00 Tues-Fri and 10:00 Sat and Sun.
14. **Fat Joe's Kitchen and Arcade:** A place where beer and fun collide. This Oceanside-owned and operated establishment is a great place to have a little fun while you're enjoying good food created with fresh ingredients. Daily specials on draft beer combined with friends and a challenging mini bowling game, Mario kart, or pinball.
15. **Valle:** Located beachfront in the Mission Pacific Resort this restaurant celebrates the flavors of the Guadalupe Valley wine region with the culinary expertise of Chef Roberto Alcocer

breakfasts and coffee houses

1. **Stratford at the Harbor:** American breakfast classics and delicious lunches served in a beach cafe along the harbor. Enjoy the fresh Ocean breezes and stroll the harbor after your fill your stomachs. Dine in or take out.
2. **Buccaneer Cafe:** American Beach front outdoor picnic table dining. Breakfasts to delight your appetite while the sun shines upon your face. Relax and watch the surf at Buccaneer Beach while you sip your specialty coffee created at the coffee bar. The espresso bar opens at 7:00 am, and the cafe opens at 8:00 am, rain or shine.
3. **Beachbreak Cafe:** This surf-inspired diner is open for breakfast and lunch. Here you are welcome to enjoy some coffee while you visit

with friends as you anticipate the moist, cinnamon-laced coffee cake topped with icing when you are seated at your table.

4. **Don's Country Kitchen:** Famous for their homestyle breakfasts and lunches prepared with locally sourced meats, fruits, and vegetables. Renowned for the Best Biscuits and gravy in town, Don also serves craft beers, cocktails, and specialty coffees. Call ahead to reserve a table on a busy weekend.
5. **Petite Madeleines:** A beautiful stroll from the Oceanside pier, this made-from-scratch fare will delight your taste buds. Choose from quiche, classic egg dishes, or something sweet but plan to take some desserts home for later.
6. **Parlor Donuts**: This unique donut shop, located north of the pier, is a must-try in Oceanside. The maple bacon layered donut melts in your mouth, as do all of the donuts in this parlor. For Gluten sensitive, Vegan, or those in need of Keto friendly, you'll find something for all here.
7. **Swami's**: Fresh food and Swami's all organic roasted coffee beans provide the perfect combo in this friendly beach cafe.
8. **Banana Dang:** Craft coffees and Smoothie bar serving fresh baked goods and Happy Toast.
9. **Switchboard:** Hawaiian Style food in the historic Finn Boutique Hotel on Coast Highway. Named to honor the women who ran the switchboard in this hotel during WWII.

Delicious cuisine is offered at 6:30 am daily. I hear the burgers are delicious.

10. **Vigilante Coffee:** With a few dollars and a passion for roasting coffee in 2014, Vigilante founder Chris launched his dream to roast award-winning coffees. This successful operation has expanded into S.O'side, where you can relax and sip organic coffee. Send a pound to your loved ones via the online portal. 1575 S Coast Hwy.

11. **Bound Coffee House:** The love of coffee and their marriage bound this couple to start the venture of craft coffee in S.O'side. The espresso drinks are made with the best beans and house-created syrups. If you want to add a homemade bite, try the freshly prepared scones, or try a breakfast burrito for something heavier. You can order online via the website. 2110 S. Coast Highway Suite. C

12. **Revolution Roasters:** Located on PCH in South Oceanside, this coffee house provides locally roasted coffees in various flavors sure to wake you up. 836 S. Coast Highway

13. **Seaborne Coffee;** Located in a renovated 1930's gas station along with a coop of merchants, Seaborne serves coffees and specialty crafted drinks, including Boba, Nitro, and Kombucha. 332 S Coast Hwy

14. **Camp Coffee Company:** Inspired by the love of camping and waking up to a delicious cup

of coffee, this shop blends freshly roasted beans with an ambiance sure to refresh your memories. 101 N Cleveland St <u>C</u>
15. **Captainsgrounds:** This family-run shop serves coffee roasted a block away, ensuring you drink the best coffee. Recline in the covered outdoor patio to recharge your batteries and your cellular phone too. If you're hungry, try a leisurely breakfast such as Acai bowls or pastries from Cie Bakery.

breweries and bars

Once considered a raunchy sailors' town filled with brothels and beer, O'side bid farewell to the brothels, but the booze is bountiful and flows freely at the Bars.

1. **Bagby:** Award-winning American Beer, this familyrun establishment will satisfy your need for a brew. The food is delicious too.
2. **.Pacific Coast Spirits and Kitchen.** This small batch craft distillery uses local ingredients to create flavorful craft spirits along with California comfort food.
3. **Stone Brewing Company:** After a day of surfing,
Stone Brewing's outdoor fire-rock communal table

is the perfect way to sip a local brew while recounting your day's adventures. Bring in your favorite grub to pair with your favorite Stone Brew. Leashed pets are welcomed.

4. **Black Plague Brewing:** Award-winning brews crafted with passion and delivered in the tap room to create Oceanside friendships.

5. **Bottlecraft:** Bottlecraft is a craft beer shop, tasting room, and bar. With passion and knowledge, they curate the best hard-to- find small-batch brews. They will indeed have something to satisfy your tastes.

6. **Belching Beaver Brewery**: Craft beer made for all palates, be it an easy blond or an Imperial Stout, Belching Beaver has it all.

7. **Breakwater Brewing Co:** Between the 12-18 homebrews or 25 guest beers, you are sure to find something here to enjoy. Pizza, famous wings, and fresh salads fill your belly while the kids enjoy the video games.

8. **Legacy Brewing Company:** Legacy brewing was started to encourage friendships while enjoying the award winning beers that blend old and new flavors. Karaoke and live music are often happening here. Check the schedule for specifics.

9. **Northern Pine Brewing:** The brewers of this fine craft beer share their love of the outdoors, and memories of growing up in the Pacific Northwest and Atlantic North East are expressed through their creations. Live music performed by visiting artists adds to the enjoyment at Northern Pine.

10. **Craft Coast Beer and Tacos:** Hand-crafted beer and classic "Taco Man" tacos served in a casual beach environment. Dogs are welcome. Online ordering is another option.
11. **Oceanside Brewing Company:** Old school brewing with new school flavors combines to create a tasty brew and fun environment reflective of Old O'side good times. Two stages host comedy, music, and DJs along with local art talent. Click on their website for more specifics.
12. **Orfila Vineyards Tasting Room:** Tues-Sunday 12:00 pm-8:00 pm (9:00 pm weekends) Taste the award-winning wines produced from Orfila's own San Diego County estate and varietals from France, Italy, and Central California. Pair with bites as suggested by the chef created for the tasting room located in downtown Oceanside. Enjoy live music on select summer evenings.
13. **The Millers Table:** Wooden tables and farmhouse lighting set the tone for wine tasting provided by the owner, chef, and Sommelier, Staci Miller. Pairings of food to accompany flights of wine will delight you and your friends in this intimate, relaxed rustic venue.
14. **Coombers Craft Wines:** Bring your friends and your dog to this So. Cal. winery in downtown Oceanside. You will enjoy house wines from the finest selection of grapes offering bold flavor in every sip. Live Bands will rock you on special evenings.

notes
. . .

golf courses

...

FROM THE CLASSIC golf course to laid-back beach-vibed short courses, O'side has something fun, affordable, and family-friendly for visitors.

1. **Arrowood:** Par-71, 18 holes, 6,721-yard layout.cated on the hilltop above the San Louis Rey Valley creates an open and unconfined feel for golfers. Ocean breezes will challenge you on the last four holes dubbed "The Quandary."
2. **Oceanside Municipal Golf Course**: Par 72, 18 holes, 6480 Yards This course is adjacent to Camp Pendleton and is minutes away from Downtown

    Oceanside. It boasts stunning views of the San Luis Rey Valley, where hillsides provide a protected habitat for various birds and wildlife native to So. Cal. This nicely maintained and challenging course won't break your vacation budget but will provide lots of fun. Walking is encouraged but, carts are available on a first-come, first-serve basis. If you want to work on your long game first, tee it up on the grass driving range.

Pocket Guide to Oceanside

3. **Emerald Isle Golf**: Par 56, 18 holes, 2,400 yards This executive course is a great place to enjoy golf with all your friends and family, regardless of skill level. Even experienced golfers will navigate some challenges as they play at this fun, friendly, and affordable course. To warm up, hit a few balls at the grass driving range, jump in a new golf cart and grab some food as you spend an enjoyable day at this Gem of a course.
4. **Goat Hill Park:** Par 65, 4582 (from the Back Tees), 18hole short course. Goat Hill is not your average short course. It provides challenging par 3's, multiple picturesque par 4's, and one dogleg par 5. The hills will give you a workout, but golf carts are available. This kid-friendly course allows parents and kids to develop their love of the sport free at "The Playground," 3 mini short holes family fun area. You will have a hard time finding a more challenging short course with as many unique holes anywhere in the country.
5. **Marine Memorial Golf course:** Par 72, 18 hole, 6,865 yards Plan ahead to play the Marine as you challenge yourself, reflecting on our heroes and the traditions and freedoms they fought to maintain. It is a minimum of a one-

week processing time for base access. Apply via the site below.

notes

. . .

things to do

. . .

. . .

market day

THURSDAYS ARE special days in O'side. Just past hump day not quite Friday is Market day. Start your morning at the Farmers market. Grab some food for lunch and plan to return in the evening for Sunset Market. Here you can watch the sunset as you listen to music and eat from one of many delicious vendors.

Farmers Market: Thursday 9:00 am-1:00 pm
Produce, flowers, nursery items, baked bread and mouth-watering sweets.

Sunset Market: Thursday 5:00 pm - 9:00 pm. Beautiful artisan crafts, clothes, and delicious food accompanied by music and the beautiful sun setting over the Pacific Ocean.

visit mission san luis rey

San Luis Rey de Francia, the eighteenth mission in the California Chain, founded in 1798, became the most prosperous of all the California missions. Visit to learn the history of this Mission and experience trials of the Native American Indians and the Franciscan Friars as they helped develop Oceanside. It is located 9 miles from downtown Oceanside on the San Louis Rey River. You may want to travel along the bike trail to enjoy nature before your self-guided tour through the Mission's history.

cruise bike trails

- San Luis Rey Trail: This 7.2 mile trail from the Harbor entrance on Pacific St to the mission is a nicely paved trail suited for all cyclists.

- Coastal Rail Trial: Eventually this trail will span 44 miles from Oceanside to San Diego along the coaster commuter train tracks, but as of now it picks up and drops off in various areas in Oceanside Solana Beach, and Encinitas. It is a great trail to escape some of the traffic on Pacific Coast Highway through Oceanside. It runs on the west side of the train tracks from Tyson Street to Oceanside Blvd and picks up again at Morse street to Vista Way.

take a hike

- **Guajome Regional Park Trail:** Guajome Regional
  Park is located in the coastal community of Oceanside. Some 4.5 miles of multi-use, nonmotorized trails meander through diverse Southern California habitats such as woodlands, scrub, wetlands, and mixed grasslands. Two ponds attract migratory birds and serve as home to a variety of fish that will test the skills of any angler

- **Lake Buena Vista:** Enjoy the 1/4 mile nature trail that loops around the Buena Audobon Society. A variety of native plants and habitats are represented, which are planted and maintained by the Native Plant Club. Use the smartphone-friendly interactive online mapping program to help identify plants and key features along the trail. Location:2202 S. Coast Highway

- **Calavera Mountain and Trail:** Access these trails via Oak Riparian Park, a public park connecting over 6.4 miles of trails via Carlsbad's Calavera Trail System, which will connect you to the Lake Calavera Trails. Dogs on leash are welcome, as are mountain bikes. The main trail has numerous smaller trails that split off in lots of directions.

Location: Oak Riparian Park 4625 Lake Blvd,

View from the top of Mt. Calavera

- **El Corazon Creek Trail:** (El Corazon Nature Trail) This one-mile easy walking nature trail is great for exploring with the kids. A wide inviting trail of rolling hills, birds, and wildlife, with lovely sights around each bend. Monday – Friday 7:30 am – 5:00 pm and Saturdays 8 am – 4 pm. Location: 3210 Oceanside Boulevard, Oceanside, CA 92057

- **The San Luis Rey River Trail:** This Class I bicycle trail is open to pedestrians as well. The trail is 7.2 miles, one way, from the Neptune access (west end) to the eastern-most point on the College Bridge. The trail follows the path to the San Luis Rey River. Walkers and runners are welcome to bring "their dogs to the trail for exercise as well.

Location: Access Point 1, the westernmost entrance, is located on Neptune Way in downtown Oceanside. Access Point 10, the easternmost entrance, is located on North Santa Fey Avenue and Highway 76. San Luis Rey

Annies Canyon Trail: Although not located in Oceanside or neighboring Carlsbad, this unique trail will lead you to a slot canyon path created by thousands of years of erosion. The Vista at the top provides views of the Pacific Ocean and Central Basin. There are two ways to get to the top vista but the canyon slot provides unforgettable geology. Going through the canyon is one way and requires some climbing. Another way to get to the vista is to hike up the switchback which is a moderate incline.

Location: 2 ways to approach Annies Canyon (google directions in Maps)

1. Solana Hills Trail Head entrance. 1.6 mi loop
2. N.Rio Ave 1.4 mi loop:

Entering Annies Canyon

Mull around a museum

Oceanside Museum of Art: Downtown museum featuring local So. Cal artists. Several yearly exhibitions and art auctions.**Oceanside Museum of Art**

Surf Museum: Learn the history of surfing surfboards and wave riding in this 30+-year-old surf museum. **Surf Museum**

notes

...

goodbye and please come again

. . .

OCEANSIDE, first developed by the Franciscans as they built Mission San Luis Rey, has maintained its old beach charm. It remains here to provide you with a fantastic warm Southern California getaway. Enjoy the attractions of San Diego with the laidback vibes of this coastal community all within 35 miles of San Diego. From harbor fishing, beach biking, surfing, or trail hiking you are sure to experience a great day in O'side. Finish your day with a delightful bar hop culminating with an amazing dinner by one of the many superior chefs in Oceanside. I hope this travel pocket guide was informative and ignites your travel desire to visit us here in Oceanside. Let's get together on the beach or maybe at a restaurant. Until we meet, I wish you happiness, sunshine, and peace. Jeanine

bibliography

333 Pacific. (n.d.). Cohnrestaruants. Retrieved July 13, 2022, from https:// www.cohnrestaurants.com/333pacific

Amtrak. (n.d.). Amtrak. Retrieved July 7, 2022, from https://www.amtrak. com/regions/california.html

Angels Ballpark. (n.d.). Https://Www.Mlb.Com/Angels/Ballpark. Retrieved July 12, 2022, from https://www.mlb.com/angels/ballpark

Anitas. (n.d.). Anitas Mexican Food. Retrieved July 13, 2022, from https:// anitasmexicanfoodrestaurant.com/

Arrowood golf. (n.d.). Arrowood. Retrieved July 12, 2022, from https:// arrowoodgolf.com/

Bagby beer. (n.d.). Bagby Beer. Retrieved July 20, 2022, from https://www. bagbybeer.com/

Balboa Park. (n.d.). Balboa Park. Retrieved July 12, 2022, from https://www. balboapark.org/

Bananadang. (2015, January 1). Bananadang. Retrieved July 12, 2022, from http://bananadang.com/

Beachbreak cafe. (2018, January 1). Beachbreak Cafe. Retrieved July 9, 2022, from https://beachbreakcafe.net/

Belching Beaver. (n.d.). Belching Beaver. Retrieved July 20, 2022, from https:// oceanside.belchingbeaver.com/

The Best Western Plus Oceanside Palms. (n.d.). Best Western Hotels. Retrieved July 9, 2022, from https://www.bestwestern.com/content/best-western/ en_US/booking-path/hotel-details.05713.html?propertyCode=05713& cm_mmc=BL-_-Google-_-GMB-_-05713

Black plague brewing. (n.d.). Black Plague. Retrieved July 20, 2022, from https://blackplaguebrewing.com/

Blade 1936. (n.d.). Blade 1936. Retrieved July 12, 2022, from https://www. blade1936.com/

Boats 4 Rent. (n.d.). Boats 4 Rent. Retrieved July 9, 2022, from https://boat s4rent.com/oceanside/

Booking.com Hotels Oceanside. (n.d.). Booking. Retrieved July 9, 2022, from https://www.booking.com/searchresults.en-us.html?aid=1430043&label= VR-SR-DL-desktop-c200-76873064-4be8-cf80-b717-b64f80e61eb2&sid= fcb9e869642ee9557dfecf5f624b9c1c&checkin=2022-08-

Bibliography

    27&checkout=202209-
    05&class_interval=1&dest_id=20014909&dest_type=city&dtdis
    c=0&
    inac=0&index_postcard=0&keep_landing=1&label_click=undef
    &offset=0&
    postcard=0&raw_dest_type=city&room1=A%2CA&sb_price_ty
    pe=total&
    shw_aparth=1&slp_r_match=0&ss_all=0&ssb=empty&sshis=0&
    utm_medium=partner&utm_source=aff_cj&

Bottlecraft. (n.d.). Bottlecraft. Retrieved July 20, 2022, from https://bottlecraft.com/

Bound Coffee. (n.d.). Bound Coffee. Retrieved July 15, 2022, from https://www.boundbycoffee.net/

Breakwater brewing. (n.d.). Breakwater Brewing. Retrieved July 20, 2022, from https://breakwaterbrewing.com/

Buccaneer cafe. (n.d.). Buccaneer Cafe. Retrieved July 9, 2022, from https://www.buccaneer-cafe.com/

    Calavera trails. (n.d.). Carlsbad California.
    https://www.carlsbadca.gov/depart ments/parks-recreation/lagoons-
    trails-openspace/trails/lake-calavera

California census. (n.d.). California Census. Retrieved July 7, 2022, from https://www.census.gov/quickfacts/CA

California Kahuna Surfschool. (n.d.). California Kahuna. Retrieved July 9, 2022, from http://www.cakahuna.com/

California surf museum. (n.d.). Surf Museum. Retrieved July 19, 2022, from https://surfmuseum.org/

Camp coffee company. (2022, July 19). Camp Coffee Company. Retrieved July 19, 2022, from https://campcoffeecompany.com/

Captains grounds. (n.d.). Captains Grounds. Retrieved July 19, 2022, from https://www.captainsgroundscoffee.com/

Carte blanche. (n.d.). Carte Blanche. Retrieved July 13, 2022, from https://www.eatcarteblanche.com/

Coastal trail. (n.d.). Traillink. https://www.traillink.com/trail/coastalrailtrail/

Coomber. (n.d.). Coombers. Retrieved July 12, 2022, from https://www.coomberwines.com/

Coronado Visitor Center. (n.d.). Https://Coronadovisitorcenter.Com/. Retrieved July 12, 2022, from https://coronadovisitorcenter.com/

Craftcoast. (n.d.). Craftcoast. Retrieved July 20, 2022, from https://craftcoast.co/

Del Mar Thoroughbred Racing Club. (n.d.). Del Mar Thoroughbred Racing Club. Retrieved July 9, 2022, from https://www.dmtc.com/

DelMar Fair. (n.d.). Del Mar Fair and Races. Retrieved July 9, 2022, from https://delmarfairgrounds.com/

Disneyland. (n.d.). Disneyland. Retrieved July 12, 2022, from https://disneyland.disney.go.com/destinations/disneyland/?CMP=OKC330339_G M_DLR_destination_disneylandpark_NA

Dons country kitchen. (n.d.). Don's Country Kitchen. Retrieved July 9, 2022, from https://donscountrykitchen.com/

Bibliography

Emerald isle golf. (n.d.). Emerald Isle Golf. Retrieved July 20, 2022, from https://www.emeraldislegolf.net/

Farmers market. (n.d.). Mainstreet Oceanside. Retrieved July 19, 2022, from https://www.mainstreetoceanside.com/farmers-market

Fish Taxi. (n.d.). Fish Taxi. Retrieved July 9, 2022, from https://fishtaxi.com/

Flying pig. (n.d.). Flying Pig. Retrieved July 12, 2022, from https://flyingpig.pub/

The Fynn Hotel Oceanside. (n.d.). The Fynn. Retrieved July 9, 2022, from https://www.thefinhoteloceanside.com/

Gaslamp district San Diego. (n.d.). Gaslamp District San Diego. Retrieved July 10, 2022, from https://www.gaslamp.org/

Goat hill golf. (n.d.). Goat Hill Golf. Retrieved July 20, 2022, from https://goathillpark.com/

Guajome trail. (n.d.). San Diego Parks. https://www.sdparks.org/content/ sdparks/en/park-pages/Guajome.html

Helgren Sportfishing. (n.d.). Helgren Sportfishing. Retrieved July 9, 2022, from https://www.helgrensportfishing.com/

Hello Betty. (n.d.). Hello Betty. Retrieved July 13, 2022, from https://www. hellobettyoceanside.com/

Honda Center. (n.d.). Honda Center. Retrieved July 12, 2022, from https:// www.hondacenter.com/

The Hotel Oceanside. (n.d.). The Hotel Oceanside. Retrieved July 8, 2022, from https://www.thehoteloceanside.com/

Bibliography

Knotts berry farm. (n.d.). Knotts Berry Farm. Retrieved July 12, 2022, from https://www.knotts.com/

The Lab collaborative. (n.d.). The Lab Collaborative. Retrieved July 12, 2022, from https://thelabcollaborative.com/

Lake Buena Vista. (n.d.). Buena Vista Audubon Society. Retrieved July 10, 2022, from https://bvaudubon.org/nature-center/https://bvaudubon.org/ nature-center/

Learn To Rip Surf Lessons. (n.d.). Learn to Rip Surf Lessons. Retrieved July 9, 2022, from https://learntoripsurflessons.com/

Learn To Surf With Heather. (n.d.). Learn To Surf With Heather. Retrieved July 9, 2022, from http://learntosurfwithheather.com/

Legacy Brewing Co. (n.d.). Legacy Brewing Co. Retrieved July 20, 2022, from http://legacybrewingco.com/

Legoland. (n.d.). Legoland. Retrieved July 9, 2022, from https://www.legoland. com/california/

Marine golf course. (n.d.). Marine Golf Course. Retrieved July 19, 2022, from https://www.mccscp.com/golf/

Mark's Surf Instruction. (n.d.). Mark's Surf Instruction. Retrieved July 9, 2022, from https://surfboardsoceanside.com/

Masters. (n.d.). Masters. Retrieved July 12, 2022, from https://www.mastersoceanside.com/

Matsu. (n.d.). Https://Eatatmatsu.Com/. Retrieved July 12, 2022, from https://eatatmatsu.com/

Metrolink. (n.d.). Metrolink. Retrieved July 8, 2022, from https://metrolink trains.com/rider-info/general-info/stations/oceanside/

Millers table. (n.d.). Millers Table. https://www.themillerstable.com/

Mission San Luis Rey. (2022, July 19). Mission San Luis Rey. https://www. sanluisrey.org/

MissionPacificHotel. (n.d.). Https://Www.Hyatt.Com/En-US/Hotel/California/Jdv-Mission-Pacific/Sanjo. Retrieved July 8, 2022, from https://www. hyatt.com/en-US/hotel/california/jdv-mission-pacific/sanjo

North County Surf Academy. (n.d.). North County Surf Academy. Retrieved July 9, 2022, from https://www.northcountysurfacademy.com/

Northern pine brewing. (n.d.). Northern Pine Brewing. Retrieved July 20, 2022, from https://www.northernpinebrewing.com/

Oceanside brewing co. (n.d.). Oceanside Brewing Co. https://www.oceansidebrewingco.com/

Oceanside Coast Expeditions. (n.d.). Oceanside Coast Expeditions. Retrieved July 9, 2022, from https://oceansidecoastalexpeditions.com/

Oceanside municipal. (n.d.). Oceanside Municipal. Retrieved July 20, 2022, from https://playoceansidegolf.com/

Oceanside museum of art. (n.d.). Oceanside Museum of Art. Retrieved July 19, 2022, from https://oma-online.org/

Oceanside Surf School. (n.d.). Oceanside Surf School. Retrieved July 9, 2022, from https://oceansidesurfschool.com/

Oceanside Whalewatching. (n.d.). Oceanside Whale Watching. Retrieved July 9, 2022, from https://www.oceansidewhalewatching.com/

OceansideMarinasuites. (2022, July 9). OmniHotels. http://www.omihotel.com/

Old town San Diego. (n.d.). Https://Oldtownsandiegoguide.Com/. Retrieved July 10, 2022, from https://oldtownsandiegoguide.com/

Orfila. (n.d.). Orfila. Retrieved July 20, 2022, from https://www.orfila.com/

Pacific coast spirits. (n.d.). Pacific Coast Spirits. Retrieved July 20, 2022, from https://paccoastspirits.com/

Pacific Venture Charters. (n.d.). Pacific Venture Charters. Retrieved July 9, 2022, from https://pacific-venture.com/private-fishing-charter-oceanside-ca/

Paradise By The Sea RV Resort. (n.d.). Paradise by the Sea. Retrieved July 8, 2022, from https://paradisebythesearvresort.com/

Parlor doughnuts. (n.d.). Parlor Doughnuts. Retrieved July 13, 2022, from https://www.parlordoughnuts.com/

Petco Park. (n.d.). Petco Park. Retrieved July 10, 2022, from https://petcoparkevents.com/

Petite madeline bakery. (n.d.). Petite Madeline Bakery. Retrieved July 13, 2022, from https://www.petitemadelinebakery.com/

Piper. (n.d.). Piper. Retrieved July 12, 2022, from https://piperoceanside.com/

The Plot. (n.d.). The Plot. Retrieved July 12, 2022, from https://theplotrestaurant.com/

Bibliography

The privateer. (n.d.). The Privateer. Retrieved July 13, 2022, from https://www. theprivateercoalfirepizza.com/

Bibliography

Revolution roasters. (n.d.). Revolution Roasters. Retrieved July 19, 2020, from https://www.revoroasters.com/

Sail Oceanside. (n.d.). Sail Oceanside. Retrieved July 9, 2022, from https:// sailoceanside.com/

San Diego Surf. (n.d.). San Diego Surf. Retrieved July 9, 2022, from https:// sandiegosurf.com/

San Diego Zoo and Safari Park. (n.d.). San Diego Zoo and Safari Park. Retrieved July 10, 2022, from https://sandiegozoowildlifealliance.org/

SeaBird. (n.d.). The Seabird. Retrieved July 8, 2022, from https://www.hyatt. com/en-US/hotel/california/jdv-mission-pacific/sanjo

Seaborne coffee. (n.d.). Seaborne Coffee. Retrieved July 19, 2022, from https:// seabornecoffee.com/

Seaworld. (n.d.). Seaworld. Retrieved July 10, 2022, from https://seaworld. com/san-diego

Springhill Oceanside. (n.d.). Springhill Suites. Retrieved July 8, 2022, from https://www.marriott.com/en-us/hotels/sanod-springhill-suitessandiego-oceanside-downtown/overview/

Sprinter schedule CA. (n.d.). Sprinter. Retrieved July 8, 2022, from http:// gonctd.com

Stonebrewing. (n.d.). Stonebrewing. Retrieved July 20, 2022, from https:// www.stonebrewing.com/

Stratford at the harbor. (n.d.). Stratford at Harbor. Retrieved July 12, 2022, from https://www.stratfordattheharbor.com/

Surfin Fire Surf School. (n.d.). Surfin Fire Surf School. Retrieved July 9, 2022, from https://surfinfire.com/

Surfride surf school. (n.d.). Surfride Surf School. Retrieved July 9, 2022, from https://www.surfride.com/

Swamis cafe. (n.d.). Swamis Cafe. Retrieved July 12, 2022, from https://www. swamiscafe.com/oceansid

Switchboard LLC, T. (2022, January 1). *The Switchboard*. The Switchboard. Retrieved July 15, 2022, from https://www. theswitchboardrestaurant.com/

Turo. (n.d.). Turo. Retrieved July 7, 2022, from https://turo.com/us/en/search?defaultZoomLevel=11&delivery=true&deliveryLocationType=airport&endDate=07%2F27%2F2022&endTime=10%3A00&is

MapSearch=false&itemsPerPage=200&latitude=32.7338&location=SAN%20-%20San%20Diego%20International%20Airport&locationType=AIRPORT&longitude=-117.1933&placeId=ChIJ7-bxRDmr3oARawtVV_lGLtw&sortType=RELEVANCE&startDate=07%2F24%2F2022&startTime=10%3A00&useDefaultMaximumDistance=true

Universal studios. (n.d.). Universal Studios. Retrieved July 12, 2022, from https://www.universalstudioshollywood.com/web/en/us

Vacation Center Oceanside. (n.d.). Vacation Rentals Oceanside. Retrieved July 9, 2022, from https://www.vacationrenter.com/search/Oceanside

Vigilante Coffee Company, T. (2022, January 1). *Vigilante coffee*. Vigilante Coffee. Retrieved July 15, 2022, from https://www.vigilantecoffee.com/

Visit California. (n.d.). Visit California. Retrieved July 3, 2022, from https:// www.visitcalifornia.com/places-to-visit/oceanside/

Visit San Diego. (n.d.). Visit San Diego. Retrieved July 12, 2022, from https:// www.sandiego.org/about/coronavirus.aspx?gclid=R0yhUmNwf3WmCpHNeWA_BbRoCOp4QAvD_BwE

VRBO. (n.d.). VRBO. Retrieved July 9, 2022, from https://www.vrbo.com/ search/keywords:oceanside-california-united-states-of-america? petIncluded=false

Where to stay. (n.d.). Visit Oceanside. https://visitoceanside.org/californiawelcome-center-oceanside/

Whitlock Surf Experience. (n.d.). Whitlock Surf Experience. Retrieved July 9, 2022, from https://whitlocksurfexperience.com/

Wrench and rodent. (n.d.). Wrench and Rodent. Retrieved July 12, 2022, from https://www.seabasstropub.com/

Bibliography

notes

Made in the USA
Las Vegas, NV
03 July 2025